Exploring English
Workbook

Hugh Templeton and Tim Blakey

Cassell

CASSELL LTD
1 St Anne's Road, Eastbourne
East Sussex BN21 3UN

© Cassell Ltd, 1984

First published 1984
Reprinted 1984 (twice), 1985
ISBN 0 304 31153 7

Illustrations by Trevor Waugh

Designed by Jacky Wedgwood

Edited by Louise Aylward

Phototypesetting by Multiplex medway ltd

Printed and bound in Hungary

Contents

Introduction

This is Book 3 in a series of four Workbooks designed to accompany Cassell's Foundation English course.

Each Workbook contains lively, interesting exercises designed specifically to give practice in the main structural, lexical and functional areas covered in the Coursebooks.

Areas of particular difficulty – such as modal and phrasal verbs – are highlighted, and all the exercises are organized on a unit-by-unit basis to facilitate their use in conjunction with the Coursebooks.

The Workbooks are equally suitable for use in class or at home; and it is hoped that the varied range of imaginative, stimulating exercises will encourage and help students to consolidate their learning in a practical and enjoyable way.

The Workbooks have been written by experienced, practising teachers, in close collaboration with the authors of the Coursebooks.

Simple Present / Present Continuous **UNIT 1**

Exercise 1 Look at the picture. Complete each sentence with the correct verb form.

1 Old Arthur _____ along a road through the woods. (walk)

2 He _____ about a mile from the village. (live)

3 The sun _____ on the trees beside the road. (shine)

4 In England, the sun _____ every day. (not shine)

5 It's a warm day, but Arthur _____ a jacket and an old cap. (wear)

6 He always _____ the same clothes, even in summer. (wear)

7 He _____ a raincoat. (not have)

8 When it _____ , he _____ at home. (rain / stay)

Exercise 2 Old Arthur sometimes goes to the village pub. He meets people there, but he doesn't talk very much. People ask him questions and he always gives very short answers.

Here are some questions.

1 Is it raining, Arthur?
  Yes, _____ .

2 Are you married? No, _____ .

3 Do you have a girlfriend, then?
  No, _____ .

4 Are your parents still alive?
  No, _____ .

5 Do you live in the village?
  No, _____ .

6 Do you like the woods?
  Yes, _____ .

7 Are you warm enough in that jacket? Yes, _____ .

8 Does your hut have a bathroom?
  No, _____ .

9 Does the postman visit you?
  No, _____ .

10 Are we asking too many questions? Yes, _____ .

Use the table to give Arthur's answers.

I	am
you	'm not
he	
she	is
it	isn't
we	are
they	aren't
	do
	don't
	does
	doesn't

UNIT 1

Exercise 3

Look at the picture. Peter is at work.
What's he doing?
Form questions from the table below.
The answers to your questions are
given under the spaces you write in.

What Where Who Why	is Peter	doing with the parcels? examining? taking things out of the bag? putting the unwrapped parcels? reporting to? wearing round his neck?

1 _____ ?

A carrier bag.

2 _____?

A microphone.

3 _____?

Because it's making a ticking sound.

4 _____?

He's unwrapping them.

5 _____?

On the floor beside him.

6 _____?

To his commanding officer.

Exercise 4

Look at the picture. Make three sentences about the picture with the words below.

1 Some Jamaicans / live / in Albion Street.

_____.

2 Two women / walk / down the street.

_____.

3 Mr Curtis / clean / his car.

_____.

Look at the picture again. The following sentences are not true. Make the sentences negative.

4 Mr Curtis owns a fish and chip shop.

_____.

5 Albion Street is a motorway.

_____.

6 The houses in the street all look the same.

_____.

7 London streets are always very wide.

_____.

8 In England, you drive on the right.

_____.

UNIT 1

Exercise 5 Complete the text with the words in the list. You can use each word only once.

always because beer buys collect corner drinks listens post village

Old Arthur has a friend called Harry. Harry lives in the [1]_____ near the church. He and Arthur usually meet once a week in the [2]_____ office. They go there to [3]_____ their pension. When they come out, they [4]_____ go straight across the road and into the pub.

They usually sit in a [5]_____ beside the fire with two pints of [6]_____ on the table in front of them. There is never any argument about paying for the [7]_____ . Arthur [8]_____ the first two pints and Harry pays for the next two. Harry talks a lot more than Arthur [9]_____ he has many friends in the village. Arthur sits quietly beside him. He [10]_____ carefully to every conversation and watches the faces around him.

Simple Present or Present Continuous? Present Continuous as a Future

UNIT 2

Exercise 1

Cathy is phoning a friend. She is
talking about her wedding. She is
getting married in the summer.
What does Cathy say?
Make sentences with these words.

1 We / get married / the local church.

   _____ .

2 We / invite / 200 people / wedding.

   _____ .

3 Father Francis / conduct / the service.

   _____ .

4 My brother / play / the organ / the wedding.

   _____ .

5 We / have / the wedding reception / the Majestic Hotel.

   _____ .

6 We / drive / reception / a Rolls Royce.

   _____ .

7 My father / pay for / everything.

   _____ .

8 Steve and I / go / Spain for our honeymoon.

   _____ .

UNIT 2

Exercise 2

Here is a page in Cathy's diary for next week.

MONDAY	Driving Lesson 6.30 – 8.30 p.m.	THURSDAY	Shopping all day with Aunt Phyllis. Film in the evening
TUESDAY	Playing Tennis with Mark. Meet at club at 7.00 p.m.	FRIDAY	Meet Steve at Kings Cross Station. Train arrival from York 8.40 p.m.
WEDNESDAY	Mustn't miss 'Dallas' on T.V. (9.15 p.m.)	SATURDAY	Steve and I invited to dinner with Mark.
		SUNDAY	Take Steve to Kings Cross Station at 8.30 p.m.

Cathy's friend wants to arrange a meeting next week. Give Cathy's answers to her questions.

Example Can we meet on Monday evening?
CATHY Oh, I'm having a driving lesson on Monday evening.

1 Well, what about Tuesday evening?

_____ .

2 And Wednesday evening?

_____ .

3 Well, Thursday, then?

_____ .

4 What are you doing on Friday night?

_____ .

5 Are you free on Saturday evening?

_____ .

6 And Sunday?

_____ .

6

Exercise 3   Put the verbs enclosed in brackets into the correct present tense.

It _____ (not snow)[1] a lot in London, but this morning it _____ (snow)[2] heavily. The traffic _____ (move)[3] very slowly because the roads _____ (be)[4] very icy. David usually _____ (go)[5] to work by bus, but today he _____ (walk)[6] because the buses _____ (not run)[7] on time. He _____ (wear)[8] his winter coat and a thick scarf but he _____ (not like)[9] this kind of weather.

David _____ (work)[10] in the local library. He _____ (be)[11] the chief librarian. When he _____ (arrive)[12] at work this morning, he _____ (interview)[13] a new assistant librarian.

Exercise 4   Make questions from the table. The answers to your questions are under the spaces that you write in.

Who What Where Why When	do are	you	going to the party with? learning English? like for breakfast? selling your car? start work? washing your hair?

1 _____?

I'm getting a new one next month.

2 _____?

At a private school.

3 _____?

At 9 o'clock every morning.

4 _____?

I'm going out tonight.

5 _____?

Black coffee and a piece of toast.

6 _____?

With some friends from school.

UNIT 3 Simple Past

Exercise 1

Do you remember what happened to Henri on the bus? The story is on page 14 of *Exploring English*. Read it again.

Complete each sentence with the past simple form of the verb.

1 Henri _____ on a bus in London. (be)

2 He _____ to get off the bus. (want)

3 He _____ the bell twice. (ring)

4 The bus _____ . (not stop)

5 The conductor _____ at Henri. (shout)

6 Henri _____ a word that he said. (not understand)

7 Henri _____ his landlady about the incident. (tell)

8 His landlady _____ that he should only ring the bell once. (explain)

Exercise 2

You are Henri's landlady. You are asking Henri about the incident on the bus yesterday. Make six sentences from the tables. (Henri's answers are given on the right of each table.)

Did	the bus the driver the conductor you	explain that you were a foreigner? get annoyed with you? stop at the next bus stop?	1 Yes, he did. 2 Yes, it did. 3 No, I didn't.

Why Where	did didn't	you	get off? ring the bell twice? understand the conductor?	4 I wanted to make sure the driver heard me. 5 At the next stop. 6 He spoke so fast.

1 _____ ?

2 _____ ?

3 _____ ?

4 _____ ?

5 _____ ?

6 _____ ?

Exercise 3 Each sentence describes what Maria does every morning. Rewrite each sentence in the past simple tense. Begin each sentence with 'Yesterday ...'

1 Maria gets up at half past seven.

   Yesterday _____ .

2 She goes downstairs before Mrs Robinson is awake.

   Yesterday _____ .

3 She has coffee for breakfast but Mrs Robinson wants a cup of tea.

   Yesterday _____ .

4 She takes Mrs Robinson her tea in bed.

   Yesterday _____ .

5 She leaves the house at half-past eight.

   Yesterday _____ .

6 She comes back to the house at five o'clock.

   Yesterday _____ .

Exercise 4 All these verbs are in Unit 3. Write down the missing form of each verb.

Present Simple	Past Simple	Present Simple	Past Simple
bring			paid
	fell	put	
give			said
	went	speak	
hear			stopped
	lay	stand	
lose			told

UNIT 4   Simple Past with AGO

Exercise 1   Here is a *curriculum vitae*.

NAME	Sheila Knight
SEX	Female
STATUS	Married (1976)
DATE OF BIRTH	24/9/39
PLACE OF BIRTH	Cardiff, Wales
EDUCATION	
1945–1951	Tydraw Primary School
1951–1957	Llandaff Grammar School
1958–1961	Bristol University
EXAMINATIONS	1957 – A level: French, German, English
	1961 – BA degree: French and English
WORK EXPERIENCE	
1962–1965	French teacher at Wandsworth Comprehensive School in London
1965–1969	English Language teacher in private language school in Reykjavik, Iceland
1969–1974	Lecturer in English, Salonika University, Greece
1975–	Director of Anglocentre School of English, Portland, England

Make sentences from these words.

1 Sheila Knight / born / Cardiff / 1939.

_____   .

2 went / Tydraw Primary School / 1945 / 1951.

_____   .

3 got / 'A' levels / at school in French …

_____   .

4 left / Grammar School / 1957 and became / university student / 1958.

_____   .

5 study French / English / University / but / study German.

_____   .

6 when / left / University / became / teacher at …

_____   .

7 changed / job in 1965 / / worked abroad / 1965 / 1974.

_____   .

8 Director of Anglocentre School of English / 1975 / married / 1976.

_____   .

Exercise 2

When did the Second World War end?
This question can be answered in two ways.

A *It ended in* 1945.
B *It ended* (thirty-eight) *years ago.*

Now give two answers to each of these questions.

1 When did the Second World War start? (1939).

A _____ .

B _____ .

2 When did the first atom bomb fall on Hiroshima? (1945).

A _____ .

B _____ .

3 When was Mount Everest climbed for the first time? (1953).

A _____ .

B _____ .

4 When was the first space flight with a human astronaut? (1961).

A _____ .

B _____ .

5 How long ago was President Kennedy assassinated? (1963).

A _____ .

B _____ .

6 How long ago was the first landing on the moon? (1969).

A _____ .

B _____ .

Exercise 3

Answer these questions with complete sentences. Use the word AGO.

1 When were you born?

_____ .

2 When did you start learning English?

_____ .

3 When did you first see *Exploring English*?

_____ .

11

4 When was your last birthday?

_____ .

5 How long ago did you wash your hair?

_____ .

6 How long ago did you go to a dentist?

_____ .

7 When was your last holiday?

_____ .

8 Have you had your breakfast yet?

_____ .

Exercise 4 Complete the text with the words in the list. You can use each word only once.

didn't   education   famous   in   left   lived   married   started   until   writer

William Shakespeare was born in Stratford-on-Avon [1]_____ 1564. His father was a glove merchant and his mother came from a rich family who [2]_____ near the town. He had a good [3]_____ at the local school.

In 1582, William [4]_____ Anne Hathaway, the daughter of a family friend. He probably worked as a school teacher before he [5]_____ Stratford to go to London about 1584. In London, he came to know many writers and [6]_____ to write poems and plays. In 1594, he joined a theatre company as an actor and a [7]_____ . In May 1599, the Company moved to the [8]_____ Globe Theatre on the River Thames. Many of Shakespeare's best plays were performed here [9]_____ the theatre burnt down in 1613. Shakespeare [10]_____ live for very long after this incident. He retired to Stratford and died in 1616.

Some / Any / No / A Little / A Few
How Much / How Many

UNIT 5

Exercise 1

Look at the picture. Complete the sentences with the words in the list. You can use each word only once.

some   any   no   somebody   anybody   nobody   something   anything   nothing

1   When Frank goes fishing, he always takes _____ with him.

2   They go fishing very early in the morning when _____ is about.

3   There are _____ cows in the meadow by the river.

4   This morning, Frank caught a Silver Bream but his friend didn't catch

_____ .

5   They stopped fishing when the sun came up and had _____ to eat.

6   As the day gets warmer, it gets more difficult to catch _____ fish.

7   The fish go into deeper water and _____ will bring them to the surface.

8   There is _____ point in fishing in this river after 10.00 am.

9   Do you know _____ who goes fishing before breakfast?

UNIT 5

Exercise 2   Frank's wife is called Mary. While Frank was out fishing, Mary went shopping. Here is what she bought.

Ask questions from the tables. Mary's answers are given.

```
1 Loaf of Bread
½ Kg of Butter
6 Eggs
1 packet of Biscuits
1 Kg of Cheddar Cheese
2 Kg of Sugar
2 bottles of Milk
```

How many much	. . .	did you get?	Mary's answers
			1 Half a dozen.
			2 Two bottles.
			3 Two kilos.

Did you get …?	Mary's answers
	4 Yes, I got half a kilo.
	5 I bought a packet.
	6 No, we have a lot of coffee.

1 _____ ?

2 _____ ?

3 _____ ?

4 _____ ?

5 _____ ?

6 _____ ?

Exercise 3   Make these statements *negative*.

1 There is somebody at the door.

_____ .

2 I left some money on the table.

_____ .

3 We saw something in the corner.

_____ .

Make these statements *positive*.

4 There were no fish in the river.

_____ .

5 Nobody borrowed your pen.

_____ .

6 Don't give him anything to eat.

_____ .

Rewrite these sentences with the *same* meaning.

7 I didn't say anything.

_____ .

8 There's no coffee in the kitchen.

_____ .

9 I phoned but there wasn't anybody in.

_____ .

Exercise 4

Complete the text with the words in the list. You can use each word only once.

and   any   arrived   back   by   carry   in   London   port   started

The Cutty Sark is a famous sailing ship of the last century. She was built near

Glasgow in 1870 to [1] _____ tea and other goods from China to [2] _____ .

Her sister ship was called the Thermopylae.

In June 1872, these two ships [3] _____ a famous race from Shanghai

[4] _____ to London. Although the Cutty Sark left the port first, she was soon

delayed [5] _____ fog. The Thermopylae overtook her near Hong Kong. In

the Indian Ocean, the Cutty Sark lost her rudder [6] _____ a bad storm. She

had to sail to an African [7] _____ for repairs. Later, near the Equator, there

wasn't [8] _____ wind to move the ship, [9] _____ she finally

[10] _____ in London a week after the Thermopylae. The voyage from

Shanghai had taken 122 days.

UNIT 6 Adjectives and Adverbs

Exercise 1 Do you remember 'Journey to Kiel' in Unit 6 of *Exploring English*?

The adjectives and adverbs in these sentences do not describe the story correctly. Rewrite the sentences with the right adjectives and adverbs.

1 The author was travelling on a cold December afternoon.

_____.

2 His German was extremely good.

_____.

3 The porter nodded patiently when he asked for the train to Kiel.

_____.

4 There were two other passengers on the train – a tall, slim woman and a man with a light brown suit.

_____.

5 The ticket collector shook his head happily when he saw the author's ticket.

_____.

6 The woman explained his mistake impatiently.

_____.

7 The second train was filled with silent schoolchildren.

_____.

8 The Schleswig-Holstein countryside was hilly.

_____.

9 In the fields, there were storks standing permanently on one leg.

_____.

Exercise 2 Rewrite these two sentences as one sentence. Use an adverb.

Example He was waiting at the bus stop. He was very patient.
Answer He was waiting patiently at the bus stop.

1 He speaks English. He is a slow speaker.

_____.

2 She examined the menu. She was very careful about it.

_____.

3 They both play the piano. They are beautiful players.

_____.

4 He retired and went to live in France. His retirement was permanent.

_____.

5 He shook my hand and thanked me. He was very grateful.

_____ .

6 He plays football. He is a professional player.

_____ .

7 He was injured in a motor accident. The injuries were bad.

_____ .

8 He is learning Russian. He is a fast learner.

_____ .

Exercise 3

Farm animals have definite characteristics.
Which animals have which characteristics?
Choose one adjective to describe each animal. You can use each word once only.

Animals		*Characteristics*	
1 bulls	_____	clever	powerful
2 cats	_____	friendly	solitary
		hard-working	stupid
3 cows	_____	patient	timid
4 dogs	_____		
5 donkeys	_____		
6 hens	_____		
7 horses	_____		
8 sheep	_____		

UNIT 6

Exercise 4 Complete this table. The first one is done for you.

Adjective	Adverb	Adjective	Adverb
bad	badly		miserably
	awfully	nice	
cosy			occasionally
	happily	terrible	
hopeful		weary	

Exercise 5 Complete the text with words from the list. You can use each word only once.

anything   behind   carefully   don't   extremely   field   impatiently
packed   stopped   wide

It was a fine, spring morning. We decided to go for a picnic. We [1]_____ the
car and set off. The roads were [2]_____ busy. Everyone else had had the
same idea as us.

'Why are you driving so slowly?' my husband asked [3]_____ .
'There's a speed limit here,' I replied.
At last, we reached the open countryside.

'Look at that beautiful [4]_____ of daffodils!'
'Where?'
'Over there.'

I looked round, but I couldn't see [5]_____ .
'Look out!' shouted my husband. We were on the wrong side of the road.

'Can't you drive more [6]_____ .'

A little later, we got trapped [7]_____ a car pulling a large caravan.
'Why don't you overtake him?'

'I can't. The road isn't [8]_____ enough.'
'Nonsense. There's plenty of space!'

I [9]_____ the car and got out.

'Why [10]_____ you drive then?'
'Don't be silly. You know I can't drive!'

Going to Future

Exercise 1 This passage is about Roy Woods, the bus conductor. Complete the text with the correct tense of the verbs in brackets. You need to use the SIMPLE PRESENT, the SIMPLE PAST, the PRESENT CONTINUOUS and GOING TO.

Roy and his wife _____ (live)[1] in Streatham in South London. Until last week, Roy _____ (work)[2] as a bus conductor. He _____ (not earn)[3] much money. Then, last week, he _____ (win)[4] the football pools. Now he is rich and he _____ (change)[5] his life style as soon as possible. He and his wife _____ (rent)[6] a furnished flat at the moment, but they _____ (buy)[7] a house. He _____ (own)[8] an old Ford car but he _____ (sell)[9] it and buy a new one. His wife says that she _____ (have)[10] driving lessons.

Exercise 2 It's the evening of 31 December.
David and his wife Sheila have made some New Year's Resolutions.

David has decided to:	*Sheila has decided to*:
drink less beer	eat less bread
give up smoking	stop buying chocolate
take more exercise	read more books
save more money	spend less money on clothes

They are talking about their resolutions.

DAVID I'm going to drink less beer. What about you?
SHEILA I'm going to eat less bread.

Continue the conversation in the same way.

DAVID _____ .

SHEILA _____ .

DAVID _____ .

SHEILA _____ .

DAVID _____ .

SHEILA _____ .

UNIT 7

Exercise 3   What are these children going to do when they leave school?

1 Peter / nurse

_____ .

2 Edward / join / army

_____ .

3 Ronnie / work / father's business

_____ .

4 Claire / take up / hairdressing

_____ .

5 Mary / study medicine

_____ .

6 Christine / not / work

_____ .

Exercise 4   Study these holiday details and the description below.

NAME	David and Sheila	The Cameron family	Maria, John, Patty and Terence
PLACE	Majorca	Italy	Portugal
MONTH	July	August	June
ACCOMMODATION	Hotel	Camp sites	Villa
ACTIVITIES	Sunbathing (Sheila) Golf (David)	Visiting art galleries (Mr and Mrs Cameron) Playing on the campsite (the children)	Windsurfing (John and Terence) Waterskiing (Maria and Patty)
TRANSPORT	Iberian Airlines	Car	British Airways
DURATION	2 weeks	3 weeks	a month

David and Sheila are going to Majorca for their holiday. They are going to stay in a hotel. Sheila intends to sunbathe while David is going to play golf. They are travelling by Iberian Airlines and they are going to stay abroad for two weeks.

Write two similar descriptions in the same way.

_____
_____
_____
_____
_____
_____
_____
_____

Exercise 5

Tony is asking Susanne some questions. Her answers are given. Find six questions for Tony to ask from the table.

How		do?	*Susanne's answers*
How		do?	1 Try and get a job in a travel firm.
What		do that?	2 I'll look in the newspapers.
When	are you going to	leave?	3 I'll rent a furnished flat.
Where		live?	4 My sister.
Who		live with?	5 Next month.
Why		work in the travel business?	6 I'd like a job dealing with people.

1 _____ .
2 _____ .
3 _____ .
4 _____ .
5 _____ .
6 _____ .

UNIT 8   Present Perfect

Exercise 1   Make eight questions from the table and answer them truthfully.

Have you ever	drunk eaten fallen flown read seen talked visited	an elephant? down the stairs? frogs legs? in a plane? New York? poison? to a film star? *War and Peace*?	Yes No	I have(n't).

1 _____

2 _____

3 _____

4 _____

5 _____

6 _____

7 _____

8 _____

Exercise 2   You have just arrived at a friend's house. She has lost her purse. She has just been shopping. Ask her questions.

Example look / shopping bag
Answer Have you looked in your shopping bag?

1 look / coat pockets

_____ ?

2 phone / shops

_____ ?

3 search / kitchen

_____ ?

4 tell / police

_____ ?

5 drop (the purse) / street

_____ ?

6 leave (the purse) / bus

_____ ?

Exercise 3   Henry's wife always makes a list every morning of the things she has to do. Here is today's list.

> Empty the kitchen bin ✓   Sew a button on Henry's shirt. ✗
> Change the bed sheets ✓   Take the car to the garage. ✗
> Post the letters ✓   Wash the dishes ✗
> Buy toothpaste and shampoo ✓   Order meat for the weekend ✗
> Phone Harriet ✓   Collect the dry cleaning ✗

Write sentences from the list.

Examples She has emptied the kitchen bin.
She hasn't sewn a button on Henry's shirt yet.

1 _____ .

2 _____ .

3 _____ .

4 _____ .

5 _____ .

6 _____ .

7 _____ .

8 _____ .

Exercise 4   Use a sentence from the table to respond to each situation described below.

I	am going to am still have just	_____	it.

1 You are typing a letter. Your boss asks if it is finished yet.

_____ .

2 Ten minutes ago, you finished washing the car. Your wife asks if you have washed it yet.

_____ .

3 You go for lunch early. When you return to the office someone asks you out for lunch.

_____ .

4　You bought a new coat this morning. A friend says: 'Is that a new coat?'

_____ .

5　Your car is always breaking down. And repairs cost a lot of money. Decide what to do about it.

_____ .

6　A friend lent you a book. He phones and asks for it back. But you haven't finished it yet.

_____ .

7　You came back from holiday last Sunday. Someone asks you why you look so healthy.

_____ .

8　You are a secretary. Your boss left the office five minutes ago and now his wife is on the phone.
　(use I'M AFRAID.)

_____ .

Exercise 5

Complete the text with the words in the list. You can use each word only once.

actress　appeared　been　by　going　had　her　never　over　part

David Irvin has ¹_____ in more than fifty films but he has ²_____ been a star in a film before. Now he is ³_____ to play in a film of one of Shakespeare's plays with Brenda Jackman, a well known film ⁴_____ . She plays the ⁵_____ of a queen and David plays ⁶_____ son, the prince. The film is going to be made in Denmark. David has never ⁷_____ to Denmark before. In his fifty films, David has been shot, drowned, burnt to death, run ⁸_____ by cars and he has even ⁹_____ his head chopped off. This time he will be killed ¹⁰_____ a poisoned sword.

Present Perfect with Since and For
Present Perfect Continuous

Exercise 1

Fred is a guardsman. Here are the details of his life in the army.

FRED SMITH (Guardsman)
joined the army 6 years ago
served in Northern Ireland in 1980 and in 1982
parachute training course (1981)
NATO exercises in Germany and Norway
served in Cyprus with United Nations forces (1979)
took part in Trooping of the Colour ceremony (1983)
guard duty outside Windsor Castle
now stationed at Windsor since last month

Answer these questions with complete sentences.

1 How long has Fred been a guardsman?

_____ .

2 How many times has he served in Northern Ireland?

_____ .

3 What course has he done?

_____ .

4 Where has he been on NATO exercises?

_____ .

5 Where has he served with UN forces?

_____ .

6 Which famous ceremony has Fred taken part in?

_____ .

7 Where has he been doing guard duty?

_____ .

8 How long has he been stationed at Windsor?

_____ .

25

UNIT 9

Exercise 2   Answer these questions truthfully. Give a short answer to question A. (Yes, I am, No I'm not etc.) Be careful with the tense in your answers to question B.

Examples

A   Have you got a car?   *Answers*   Yes, I have.
                                                                    No, I haven't.

B   How long have you had a car?   *Answers*   I have had a car │ for ...
                                                                    I have had a car │ since ...
                                                                    I haven't got a car.

1   A   Have you got a passport?

    B   How long have you had a passport?

2   A   Have you got a job?

    B   How long have you had this job?

3   A   Are you a student?

    B   How long have you been a student?

4   A   Are you married?

    B   How long have you been married?

5   A   Are you living in Britain at the moment?

    B   How long have you been in Britain?

6   A   Are you studying English?

    B   How long have you been studying English?

7 A Do you live in a flat?

   _____ .

   B How long have you been living in a flat?

   _____ .

8 A Do you wear glasses?

   _____ .

   B How long have you been wearing glasses?

   _____ .

Exercise 3 Put the verbs in brackets in either the PRESENT PERFECT or the PRESENT PERFECT CONTINUOUS tense.

1 In the last six months, I _____ (complete) two English courses.

2 Work on the new building _____ (begin).

3 Prices _____ (rise) steadily for five years and they are still rising.

4 Fred _____ (serve) in Northern Ireland and in Cyprus.

5 Flight 707 from Amsterdam _____ (just land).

6 _____ the letters _____ (arrive) yet?

7 Sheila _____ (try) to do that crossword puzzle for half an hour and she still _____ (not finish) it.

8 I got this job in 1952. I _____ (drive) lorries for more than thirty years.

Exercise 4 Write out these sentences, using the correct PERFECT tense, or the correct PAST tense, with *for, since* or *ago*.

1 This company / make / golf clubs / 1893.

   _____ .

2 They / marry / twenty-five years.

   _____ .

3 It / stop raining / half an hour.

   _____ .

4 I / work / this firm / 1976.

   _____ .

UNIT 9

5 Columbus / discover / America / 400 years.

_____ .

6 I / write / 20 letters / 10 o'clock this morning.

_____ .

7 I / put / an advertisement in the newspaper / 3 days and the telephone / ring / continually / then.

_____ .

8 I / not see / her / 5 years. She / change / completely / then.

_____ .

Exercise 5   Complete the text with the words in the list. You can use each word only once.

abroad   ago   but   for   got   himself   since   spent   then   working

Stephen has been teaching English [1]_____ five years. He left Bristol University six years [2]_____ and went on a teacher training course. He [3]_____ taught English in Italy for two years. He enjoyed [4]_____ and learnt to speak Italian quite well. He returned to Britain and [5]_____ one year looking for a good job. He joined the English Department of a large school [6]_____ he didn't like the work. He decided to go [7]_____ again. He [8]_____ a job in the Middle East where he managed to save a lot of money. [9]_____ his return, he has been [10]_____ at a language school in Oxford.

Comparatives and Superlatives

Exercise 1   Complete these sentences with the correct COMPARATIVE or SUPERLATIVE form of the word in brackets.

1 Gold is _____ (expensive) than silver.

2 A Ferrari is _____ (fast) than a Ford.

3 Carla speaks English _____ (well) than I do.

4 In fact Carla is _____ (good) student in the class.

5 Yesterday's game was _____ (exciting) I've ever seen.

6 If you do the exercise _____ (carefully) than last time, you'll probably get it right.

7 You will feel much _____ (happy) if you forget it.

8 In the Northern Hemisphere, 21 June is the _____ (long) day of the year.

Exercise 2   Change these sentences, but do not change their meaning.

Example Wednesday was hotter than yesterday.
Answer   Yesterday was not as hot as Wednesday.

1 Tennis is more interesting than basketball.

_____ .

2 Dogs are more friendly than cats.

_____ .

3 The English language is more useful than Dutch.

_____ .

4 Peter earns less than Roger.

_____ .

5 His Spanish is better than his French.

_____ .

6 The Parthenon is not as old as the Pyramids.

_____ .

7 He doesn't drive as fast as I do.

_____ .

8 The Arabian Gulf has more oil than the North Sea.

_____ .

UNIT 10

Exercise 3   All these questions are about your country. Answer them with complete sentences.

1 Which is the most popular sport?

_____ .

2 Who is the most popular singer?

_____ .

3 Are there any large industries? (Give the most important one.)

_____ .

4 Are there any mountains over 3000 metres high? Which is the highest?

_____ .

5 Name the two largest cities. Which one is larger?

_____ .

6 How near the sea do you live? (Use *less than* or *more than*).

_____ .

Complete these two sentences with *so much* or *so many*

7 In winter, there is / are ... that ... .

_____ .

8 In summer, there is / are ... that ... .

_____ .

Exercise 4   Glasgow and Edinburgh are the two largest cities in Scotland. Look at this information about the two cities.

	GLASGOW	EDINBURGH
Population	more than 1 million	about 500 000
Area	197 km^2	272 km^2
Location	west coast 22 miles from the sea	east coast 3 miles from the sea
Distance to London	394 miles	373 miles
Industry	heavy industry (shipbuilding etc)	very little (tourism etc)
University	founded in 1451	founded in 1583

Make six sentences to compare Glasgow and Edinburgh. You can use MORE/
LESS ... THAN, NOT AS ... AS, LESS ... THAN

1 _____

2 _____

3 _____

4 _____

5 _____

6 _____

Exercise 5

Complete the text with the words in the list. You can use each word only once.

and   by   extremely   finest   first   found   have   most   Scottish   which

I ^{1}_____ lived in Edinburgh for 10 years, but I only visited the Scottish
National Gallery yesterday for the ^{2}_____ time. The building itself is one
of the ^{3}_____ classical buildings in Edinburgh.

Most of the paintings are European. The ^{4}_____ famous paintings they
have are ^{5}_____ Titian, Tiepolo, Van Dyke and Rembrandt. There is also
an ^{6}_____ valuable collection of French Impressionist paintings. In one
small room I ^{7}_____ several paintings by Constable and Turner, ^{8}_____
portraits by Gainsborough and a famous ^{9}_____ painter called Raeburn.
Downstairs there is a collection of Victorian paintings ^{10}_____ show
various scenes from novels and from history.

UNIT 11 Simple Future

Exercise 1 In these conversations, put the verbs into the SIMPLE FUTURE tense.

1 PAUL   Are you seeing James this evening?

DESMOND   Yes, I _____ (give) him your message.

2 MARY   You haven't taken your pills.

DAVID   Don't worry. I _____ (take) them in a minute.

3 PHILIP   My goodness, this room is cold, isn't it?

JOHN   _____ (put) the fire on?

4 ERNEST   And what _____ (do) when you grow up?

RACHEL   I'm going to be a policewoman.

5 PETER   Are you going on holiday soon?

SHEILA   Yes, I'm afraid I _____ (not see) you again before I go.

6 NEVIL   She has an interview for a job as a manager tomorrow.

SUSAN   She's too young. She _____ (never get) the job.

Exercise 2 You want to let your flat. Someone is looking around the flat with you, but he has a lot of queries ... Answer the questions. Use the SIMPLE FUTURE tense.

1 What about the broken window? (not worry / mend it)

_____ .

2 The tap in the bathroom leaks. (fix / tap / tomorrow)

_____ .

3 Can you get the telephone connected? (go / telephone company / this afternoon)

_____ .

4 The people in the flat upstairs – when are they moving out? (not move / before next month)

_____ .

5 How do I contact you when I decide about the flat? (give you / telephone number?)

_____ .

6 The rent seems a bit high. (never find / cheaper flat / this area)

_____ .

Exercise 3 Look at this example.
Example I / buy / brown pair / black pair.
Answer I won't buy the brown pair, I'll buy the black pair.

1 They / arrive / today / tomorrow.

_____ .

2 I / have / coffee / tea.

_____ .

3 She / go / car / train.

_____ .

4 We / give / Susan / flowers / perfume.

_____ .

5 You / find it / over there / over here.

_____ .

6 He / pay / bill / now / later.

_____ .

Exercise 4 Paul and Terry are in the pub. Terry is asking questions. Paul's answers are given on the right of the tables. Write down Terry's questions.

Shall		I	buy you another drink? give you a lift?	*Paul's answers*
		we	leave now?	1 No thanks, I've got to go. 2 Yes, My appointment's at eight. 3 That would be very kind.
Who What When Where	will	he you	be at the weekend? be in the office again? do with that report I gave you? give it to? think of it?	4 Monday morning. 5 At home, I think. 6 I'll type it out for you. 7 Mr White. 8 I'm sure he'll be very pleased.

33

UNIT 11

1 _____ ?

2 _____ ?

3 _____ ?

4 _____ ?

5 _____ ?

6 _____ ?

7 _____ ?

8 _____ ?

Exercise 5   Complete the text with the words in the list. You can use each word only once.

asked   drove   forgotten   good   on   past   said   shall   won't   you

Nigel and I decided to have a break from London.

'OK,' I said 'where ¹_____ we go?'

'How about Devon?' he suggested. 'It ²_____ be very crowded at this time of year.'

'Good idea!' I ³_____ enthusiastically. 'We'll leave ⁴_____ Friday at six. I'll drive and you can read the map.'

Nigel is ⁵_____ at map-reading.

We left London at half ⁶_____ seven. Nigel had ⁷_____ to set his alarm clock. Finally we got onto the motorway.

'That's better,' I thought as we ⁸_____ at 100 kilometres per hour towards Devon.

'Nigel, where do we turn off the motorway?'

'Where's the map?' he ⁹_____ .

'I don't know,' I replied, ' ¹⁰_____ packed it.'
'Oh, blast!'he said slowly.

Auxiliaries (Modals) I

Exercise 1   Tom and Stella are looking for
somewhere to live. You are Stella.
Make suggestions from the table.
Tom's answers are given below.

		ask	a notice to put in a shop window.
		get	an advert in the newspaper.
I	can	go	at the adverts in the paper every day.
		look	my friends if they know of any flats.
We	could	put	some more information about cheap mortgages.
		write	to a flat agency.

1 _____ .

   They all live miles away.

2 _____ .

   If they find one, you have to pay them.

3 _____ .

   Yes, perhaps we should write some letters tonight.

4 _____ .

   I'll phone the advertising department tomorrow.

5 _____ .

   Does anybody ever read those notices?

6 _____ .

   OK. Get the local paper again tomorrow.

Exercise 2   Richard and Joan are talking to a travel agent. Complete the conversation with
MAY, MIGHT, CAN or COULD.

1 RICHARD _____ we ask you some questions about Finland?

2 AGENT   Of course, but I _____ not know all the answers.

3 JOAN   _____ we hire a car there?

4 AGENT   Yes, of course. You _____ get one straight away in Helsinki,
          or you _____ prefer to travel north by train and then get a car
          to visit Lapland.

5 RICHARD _____ you tell us what souvenirs we _____ like to buy?

6 AGENT   Many people buy reindeer skins, but you _____ find them a
          little expensive.

UNIT 12

Exercise 3   Write six correct sentences using this table.

I	can't couldn't 'd rather don't want to may might	be late if I don't go at once. find my socks yesterday morning. live in Australia than Canada. leave on Monday, but I doubt it. sell the car but I need the money. swim, so I don't like the sea.

1 _____

2 _____

3 _____

4 _____

5 _____

6 _____

Exercise 4   Complete the text with the words in the list. You can use each word only once.

after   be   can't   might   phone   rather   seen   to   Tom's   would

Tom and Stella have just [1]_____ an advertisement for a flat to rent. The flat seems to [2]_____ quite cheap and it is not too far away from [3]_____ office.

TOM   I can [4]_____ from the office in the morning.

STELLA   I'd [5]_____ phone tonight. The flat [6]_____ be taken by tomorrow. You know how quickly people take them. Why [7]_____ you phone now?

TOM   OK. When do you want [8]_____ see the flat? How about tomorrow evening, immediately [9]_____ I finish work.

STELLA   That [10]_____ be fine. See if you can arrange it.

Auxiliaries (Modals) II

Exercise 1   Here are some common signs. Write a sentence to show what they mean. Use *must* or *mustn't*.

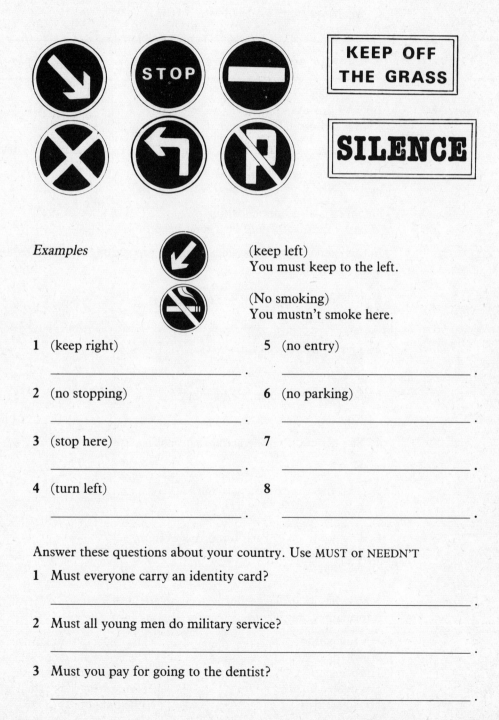

Examples

(keep left)
You must keep to the left.

(No smoking)
You mustn't smoke here.

1 (keep right)   5 (no entry)

_____ .   _____ .

2 (no stopping)   6 (no parking)

_____ .   _____ .

3 (stop here)   7

_____ .   _____ .

4 (turn left)   8

_____ .   _____ .

Exercise 2   Answer these questions about your country. Use MUST or NEEDN'T

1 Must everyone carry an identity card?

_____ .

2 Must all young men do military service?

_____ .

3 Must you pay for going to the dentist?

_____ .

UNIT 13

4 Must you have a licence to drive a car?

_____ .

5 Must you buy a licence to use a television at home?

_____ .

6 Must you get married in a church?

_____ .

Exercise 3 Look at this example.
John is in hospital for a week.

We _____ take / flowers.

Answer We ought to take him some flowers.
_or_   We'd better take him some flowers.

Ought to is _a recommendation._
'd better means _it would be a good idea to._

In this exercise, you must decide whether to use _ought to_ or _'d better_ and then
write the sentences.

1 I've just bought an expensive camera.

You _____ . insure

2 Jane's been in bed for a week.

She _____ . see / doctor

3 Someone has stolen my handbag.

You _____ . phone / police

4 Stephen didn't understand that book.

He _____ . read / again

5 This meat is extremely tough.

You _____ . call / waiter

6 I've got to go to Paris tomorrow evening.

You _____ . go / bed early

Exercise 4 Khady has an insurance form to complete for his camera. Here is the
information they want.

His full name	The make of the camera
His permanent address	The serial number of the camera
His occupation	The value of the camera
His date of birth	The address of the shop where
His signature	he bought it.

38

No,	he	'd better must mustn't needn't ought to	(...)
Yes,			

Answer the questions below by using this table.

1 Must he give the name of the shop where he bought the camera?

_____ .

2 Must he give his full name?

_____ .

3 Must he print his name in capital letters?

_____ .

4 Must he tell them where he was born?

_____ .

5 Must he insure the camera?

_____ .

6 Can he send the form back without signing it?

_____ .

7 If the camera cost £100, can he say its value is £1000?

_____ .

8 Does it matter if he doesn't complete the form now?

_____ .

Exercise 5   Complete the text with the words in the list. You must use each word only once.

can   may   might   must   mustn't   needn't   ought   rather   want

Foreign students in Britain [1]_____ usually stay with a family or they [2]_____ be able to find a cheap hotel if they'd [3]_____ be on their own. Those who [4]_____ to improve their English very quickly normally stay with a family. Students who come to Britain for more than three months [5]_____ register with the police. If you stay for less than three months, you [6]_____ register at the police station. All foreign students [7]_____ to register with a doctor although it is not compulsory. You [8]_____ need medical help during your stay. If you fall ill, you [9]_____ go directly to a hospital unless it is a serious emergency. Phone your doctor first.

UNIT 14 Simple Past v Present Perfect

Exercise 1

Doris and Belinda are walking down
the street.
You are Belinda.

1 Ask Doris how long she's been a traffic warden.

   _____.

2 Ask her how many parking tickets she's issued today.

   _____.

3 Find out what she did last night.

   _____.

4 Find out if she's had a cup of tea this morning.

   _____.

5 Find out where she bought her gloves.

   _____.

6 Find out when she started work this morning.

   _____.

Exercise 2

You are a journalist.
You're interviewing Belinda about her job.
Make questions from the table.
Belinda's answers are given under the spaces that you write in.

How much How long Where Why	do did have	you	become a traffic warden? do your training? earn at this job? known Doris? have your morning coffee? work a day?

1 _____?
Here in London.

2 _____?
Eight hours.

3 _____?
About £100 a week.

40

4 _____?

Because I didn't want to work in an office.

5 _____?

About three years.

6 _____?

At Sam's cafe.

Exercise 3   Complete these conversations.

1 A Have you ever seen the film *Casablanca*?

   B Yes, _____ .

   A When _____?

   B _____ last year.

2 A _____ ever _____ to Hong Kong?

   B Yes, _____ .

   A How _____?

   B _____ British Airways.

3 A _____ lost any money recently?

   B Yes, _____ .

   A Where _____?

   B _____ in a shop.

4 A _____ ever _____ in hospital?

   B Yes, _____ .

   A Why _____?

   B Because _____ appendicitis.

5 A _____ finished your exams yet?

   B Yes, _____ .

   A How _____ get on?

   B I don't know. I _____ my results yet.

6 A How _____ studying English?

   B Since 1980.

   A Where _____ taking lessons?

   B In a private school.

UNIT 14

Exercise 4   Here is some information about my sister.
1975   Left school
1976   Joined a firm of solicitors and studied law
1977   Passed the preliminary exams
1978   Left the solicitors and went to work for TWA
1981   Joined an international hotel group
1982   Sent to West Africa by the hotel group
1983   Working in their South American office in Rio (until present)

Answer the questions with complete sentences.

1 When did my sister leave school?

_____ .

2 How long did she study law?

_____ .

3 Which exams did she take?

_____ .

4 How many years did she work for TWA?

_____ .

5 What did she do after that?

_____ .

6 Where did the hotel group send her in 1982?

_____ .

7 And in 1983?

_____ .

8 How long has she been in Rio?

_____ .

Exercise 5   All these verbs are used in Unit 14.
Complete the table.

Verb	Past Simple	Present Perfect	Verb	Past Simple	Present Perfect
sit			break		
eat			buy		
take			read		
see			come		
win			pay		
speak			go		

Past Simple v Past Continuous

UNIT 15

Exercise 1

Eight people have been staying in the Hotel Continentale. One of them was murdered at exactly 6.30 pm last night. A detective asks each of the other guests:
'WHAT WERE YOU DOING AT 6.30 LAST NIGHT?'
Give their answers from the table.
The first one has been done for you.

Place	Activity
in the dining room	changing before dinner
in the hotel bar	eating dinner
in the garden	having a gin and tonic
in the library	playing croquet
in my room	reading the newspapers
by the swimming pool	sunbathing
in the television room	watching the news

GUEST 1   I was having a gin and tonic in the hotel bar.

GUEST 2   _____ .

GUEST 3   _____ .

GUEST 4   _____ .

GUEST 5   _____ .

GUEST 6   _____ .

GUEST 7   _____ .

Exercise 2

Look at the example.

Example Paco had his supper (at 6.30). The phone rang.
Answer Paco was having his supper when the phone rang.
or   The phone rang while Paco was having his supper.

Join the two sentences. Use WHEN or WHILE.

1 Julia had a bath (this morning). The front door bell rang.

_____ .

2 Sylvia drove to London (yesterday). She had a puncture.

_____ .

3 Liza walked down the Portabello Road (last Sunday). Someone stole her handbag.

_____ .

4 Mrs Dolphin watched Wimbledon on television (this afternoon). There was a powercut.

_____ .

5 Dr Brooks crossed the road. A motorcyclist knocked him over.

_____ .

6 The *Titanic* sailed across the Atlantic. The *Titanic* was struck by an iceberg.

_____ .

Exercise 3

There is another story in Unit 15 about a little girl on a bus.

Your friend was also on the bus and saw the incident.

Make questions from this table. Your friend's answers are given under the spaces you write in.

What Where	did was were	the little girl (she) the tall lady the other passengers	carrying? do? doing? say? sitting? wearing?

1 _____ ?

Beside her mother.

2 _____ ?

A red jumper and a blue skirt.

3 _____ ?

A blue umbrella and a crocodile handbag.

4 _____ ?

'What a funny hat!'

5 _____ ?

She gave a frozen smile.

6 _____ ?

They all thought it was very funny.

Exercise 4 Complete the text with the words in the list. You must use each word only once.

ago came could heard home learnt must nothing walking was

Many years ¹_____ , I went for a walk with a friend late at night. We were ²_____ in the hills near my home. I remember that the wind ³_____ blowing strongly that night. As we ⁴_____ to the top of the hill, we suddenly ⁵_____ the sound of a horse and its rider. We stopped and waited but ⁶_____ appeared. We decided that it ⁷_____ have been the noise of the wind in the trees. We continued our walk and eventually arrived ⁸_____ after midnight.

Some years later, I ⁹_____ that the ghost of a soldier in Charles I's army ¹⁰_____ sometimes be heard riding through those hills.

Exercise 5 Unit 15 contains a story called 'Henry's new car'. The sentences below refer to the story. Put the verbs in brackets into the correct tense – the PAST SIMPLE or the PAST CONTINUOUS.

1 Last July, Mr Jones _____ (work) in his garden one Saturday morning.

2 When the door bell _____ (ring), Mrs Jones _____ (pop) her head round the kitchen door.

3 Judy _____ (put) down her paper and _____ (go) to the front door.

4 When she _____ (open) it, Henry _____ (stand) outside.

5 He _____ (invite) them to come and look at his new car which _____ (stand) by the front gate.

6 Henry _____ (take) Judy for a little drive and _____ (come) back with her for lunch.

UNIT 16 Used to ...

Exercise 1

An old man remembers ...
Make six sentences from this table. Try to use each phrase only once.

I			be a war memorial here	before I gave it up.
			be an orchard	after the First World War.
			be much more friendly	than they are nowadays.
People	used to		have a large dog	when I was a lad.
			go fishing every Saturday morning	where those houses are.
There			smoke 40 cigarettes a day	until I moved into a small flat.

Exercise 2

Look at the example.

Example Britain/empire/EEC
Britain used to have an empire, now it's in the EEC.

Make similar sentences from these words.

1 Airliners / propellers / jet engines.

_____ .

2 Ships / sails / diesel engines.

_____ .

3 Saudi Arabia / poor country / very rich.

_____ .

4 People / listen ... radio / watch ... television.

_____ .

5 Petrol / cost less than £1 a gallon / nearly £2 a gallon.

_____ .

6 The USA / 48 States / 50.

_____ .

Exercise 3

Do you remember Susanne?

Susanne now works for a travel firm. She used to work in a shipping office but she changed her job two years ago. In the shipping office, she used to read documents and type letters all day long. Now she spends time dealing with people and she often has to go abroad on business.

She remembers the time when she used to sit behind a desk from nine o'clock to five every day. She didn't have any contact with customers and she used to get extremely bored. In those days, she used to go to work by bus, now she has a company car. She's very glad she changed her job.

Ask and answer questions about Susanne. Use *used to* in your questions and answers.

1 Where / Susanne / work?

    _____

    _____ .

2 What / do / all day long?

    _____

    _____ .

3 Why / get so bored?

    _____

    _____ .

4 How / go / work?

    _____

    _____ .

UNIT 16

Exercise 4

Do you remember your first school?
Answer the questions below from
the table.

No, Yes,	I used to I didn't use to	do like	it. them.

1 Did you do English at your first school?

_____ .

2 What about chemistry and physics?

_____ .

3 And history?

_____ .

4 Did you like the school?

_____ .

5 What about the teachers?

_____ .

6 And the other students in your class?

_____ .

Exercise 5

Complete the text with the words in the list. You can use each word only once.

anyone   grew   have   lie   only   never   saw   size   too   used

At home on the farm, we used to [1]_____ a dog called Flower. My parents [2]_____ her at a dog show and bought her for the children. We [3]_____ regretted it. When she first arrived, she was [4]_____ a few months old and she [5]_____ to chase all the cats on the farm. Of course, the cats were much [6]_____ quick for her. She [7]_____ up to be an extremely large dog who was very friendly to everyone including the cats. They used to [8]_____ on top of her in the sun. She never hurt [9]_____ , although people were often frightened by her [10]_____ and the noise she made.

To be / get used to + -ing

Exercise 1   Frank went to Zurich to learn about some new equipment.

While he was there, he had to change his life style.

Make sentences with GOT USED TO.

1 live / in a hotel ⎫
2 eat / Swiss food   ⎬ while he was in Zurich.
3 start work at 7.30 ⎭

1 _____ .

2 _____ .

3 _____ .

But there were some things Frank couldn't get used to.

Make sentences with NOT USED TO.

4 Have coffee for breakfast ⎫
5 Drive on the right   ⎬ because he's English.
6 Work nine hours a day   ⎭

4 _____ .

5 _____ .

6 _____ .

Exercise 2   Make six sentences from this table.

Air hostesses Firemen Politicians Salesmen Secretaries Sportsmen	must get used to	climbing ladders. entertaining customers. giving speeches. serving passengers. taking shorthand. training every day.

1 _____ .

2 _____ .

3 _____ .

4 _____ .

5 _____ .

6 _____ .

49

UNIT 17

Exercise 3   Make sentences with:
       IS / ARE NOT USED TO ... YET
   or HAS / HAVE GOT USED TO ... NOW

1 Pamela has just started wearing glasses.
    She finds them very uncomfortable.

    Pamela _____ not _____ wearing glasses _____ .

2 Mr White used to live in the country. Now he lives in town and he is
    beginning to like it.

    Mr White _____ got _____ now.

3 Tom is 35. He has just become a university student and he finds it very
    strange.

    Tom _____ .

4 Leila had a baby six months ago and had to leave her job. For the first three
    months she hated staying at home, but now she likes it.

    _____ .

5 George is training to be a policeman. He has to wear a uniform and he is
    still embarrassed about it.

    _____ .

6 Stella became famous very suddenly for her role in a TV play. She is
    recognised by people wherever she goes. At first it was annoying, but now
    she is quite amused by it.

    _____ .

Exercise 4

Paul Green is a young student. He only left home two months ago. Yesterday his father visited him in his new flat. Today Paul's father has to answer his wife's questions.

Make Mrs Green's questions from the table.
Mr Green's answers are given below

Has Is Will	Paul	get getting got	used to	being away from home? buying his own food? handling money? living by himself? making his own breakfast? studying at University?

1 _____?

He only has a cup of tea.

2 _____?

Yes, he has. There's a supermarket next door.

3 _____?

I'm sure he will. He's started a bank account, you know.

4 _____?

Yes, gradually. He was very lonely for the first month.

5 _____?

Yes, he is. He says it's much more interesting than school.

6 _____?

Of course he will. But he promised to visit us as often as possible.

Exercise 5

Complete the text with the words in the list. You can use each word only once.

been   born   did   flat   get   getting   move   so   used   would

Jenny has [1] _____ married for two years now. Before she got married, she [2] _____ to live with her mother. She had a job then and so her mother [3] _____ all the housework. Now she is expecting a baby and [4] _____ she has given up her job. She is [5] _____ used to housework but she says she'll never [6] _____ used to cooking. After the baby is [7] _____ , Jenny and her husband intend to [8] _____ from the town into the country. They [9] _____ like to get a house with a garden instead of the small [10] _____ they have now.

UNIT 18 Future in the Past

Exercise 1   Mr Polly didn't realise it was going to be so difficult to cut his throat.

Here are some other things Mr Polly didn't realise.
Make the sentences with WAS GOING TO.

1 his father / leave him some money.

   _____ .

2 be so difficult to run a shop.

   _____ .

3 Miriam / be so intolerable to live with.

   _____ .

4 how quickly the fire / spread.

   _____ .

5 how easy life / be without Miriam.

   _____ .

6 H.G. Wells _____ how successful his book *Mr Polly*

   _____ become.

Exercise 2   Look at the example.

Example He *was going to become* a doctor but he *became* a dentist instead.

Make six sentences from the table, using the same pattern.

I He She We You They	was were	going to	become buy go to join study visit	medicine my uncle oranges Sicily singer the army	but	apples Corsica dancer engineering my sister the navy	instead.

1 _____ .

2 _____ .

3 _____ .

4 _____ .

5 _____ .

6 _____ .

Exercise 3

Look at these two sentences.

I *knew* you weren't going to get the job!

This means:
You *didn't* get the job and I'm *not* surprised.

I thought you *weren't* going to get the job!

This means:
I *am* surprised that you *got* the job.

Make a sentence for each situation.
Use I KNEW or I THOUGHT ... YOU WERE(N'T) ...

1 Your wife has been looking for her watch for half an hour. Finally, she finds it.

   I _____ you _____ find it!

2 John took his driving test yesterday. He's a very bad driver and he wouldn't take any lessons. Naturally, he failed the test.

   _____ .

3 Susan is trying to eat her third plate of spaghetti. She gives up before she finishes.

   _____ .

4 Ted said he didn't want to play tennis today. But when you arrive at the club, there he is.

   _____ .

5 Anne promises to meet you at 6 pm. You know she is often late, but this time she promised. She arrives at 6.45 and you are very annoyed.

   _____ .

6 David said he would write a report for you last night. It is not on your desk this morning. You phone David and he tells you it isn't finished yet.

   _____ .

UNIT 18

Exercise 4   Look at these statements.

Laura got divorced last year.

If you were surprised at this news, you might ask a question like this:
'Did you have any idea she was going to get divorced?'

Make questions from the table which can follow the statements below.

Did you	have any idea know realise think	it he she they	was / were going to …?

1 Sidney had an operation last week.

   _____?

2 Mr and Mrs Green have emigrated to Australia.

   _____?

3 Susan was two hours late for my party.

   _____?

4 Henry sent me six bottles of champagne.

   _____?

5 Those books cost me £56.

   _____?

6 The journey was only 10 miles but it took us three hours.

   _____?

Exercise 5   Complete the text with the words in the list. You must use each word only once.

brought   by   going   has   novel   realises   refuses   visiting   who   whose

Henry James wrote a famous ¹_____ called *The Portrait of a Lady*. It is about a beautiful young woman who thought she was ²_____ to be very happy when she got married.

The young woman, Isabel Archer, is ³_____ to England by her aunt. She ⁴_____ already refused to marry a rich American business man ⁵_____ was sure she was going to marry him. In England, she again ⁶_____ to marry an English lord whom she meets.

While she is ⁷_____ Italy, she is introduced ⁸_____ a friend to an American living in Florence ⁹_____ name is Gilbert Osmond. She marries him but she soon ¹⁰_____ that Gilbert has only married her for her money.

UNIT 19 Past Perfect

Exercise 1   Simon is a very organised young man.
For example, here is the routine he followed when he got up yesterday.

1 He switched the radio on.
2 He combed his hair.
3 He turned the kettle on in the kitchen.
4 He laid the table for breakfast.
5 He made his bed.
6 He had a shave.
7 He had his breakfast.
8 He brushed his teeth.
9 He got dressed.

Example   (Sentences 1 and 2)
After (*or* When) he had switched the radio on, he combed his hair.

Make similar statements by combining sentences 2 and 3, sentences 3 and 4, and so on. Begin each sentence with WHEN or AFTER.

1 _____
2 _____
3 _____
4 _____
5 _____
6 _____
7 _____

Exercise 2   Helen had a party last week. Six of her friends were late for the party. They each had a different excuse.

Example George was late because he had missed his bus.

Make similar sentences about the others.

1 Stella / her mother / come to tea.

   _____.

2 Paul / someone / steal his motorbike.

   _____.

3 Stephen / get on the wrong bus.

   _____.

4 Mary / go to the theatre first.

   _____.

5 Peter / forget about the party.

   _____.

56

Exercise 3   Make questions from the table. The answers are given under the spaces you write in.

How much How long What Where Who	had you	been doing been here been staying with spent visited	before	I arrived? you bought your flat? you came to Britain? you got this job? you lost your wallet?

1 _____?

About £50.

2 _____?

Several countries in Europe.

3 _____?

I was a salesman.

4 _____?

With some friends.

5 _____?

Only about five minutes.

Exercise 4   Put the verbs in the correct tenses.

1 I _____ (met) Susan twice when I _____ (invite) her to dinner.

2 He _____ (not realise) that he _____ (lose) his passport.

3 They _____ (tell) the police that the house _____ (be) empty for a month.

4 She _____ (take) a taxi because the bus _____ (be) full.

5 The film _____ (finish) much earlier than I _____ (expect).

6 I _____ (not believe) his story until I _____ (talk) to him myself.

UNIT 19

Exercise 5   Complete the text with the words in the list. You must use each word only once.

been   could   driving   had   into   looked   realised   stood   when   where

It was a mistake to visit the house ^{1}_____ I had lived as a child.

I was ^{2}_____ through Manchester last week ^{3}_____ I decided to visit the house I was born in. I regretted it afterwards because it ^{4}_____ changed so much.

The house ^{5}_____ a lot smaller than I had remembered. Then I ^{6}_____ that the top floor and part of the back of the house had ^{7}_____ knocked down. The house had also been converted ^{8}_____ two separate flats.

I walked round to see the garden. What a change! A bungalow now ^{9}_____ where the tennis court had been and I ^{10}_____ see that the field behind had become a housing estate.

Reported Speech I

Exercise 1   Connie spoke to her father (Mr Bridges) on the telephone last night.
Here are some of the things she said.

1   I've visited London this week.
2   We've been to the British Museum.
3   We also saw the Houses of Parliament.
4   Grandmother is looking very well.
5   We are planning to go to York next week.
6   I'll send you a postcard from York.

Connie's father reports these sentences to his wife, Connie's mother. Write
down the six sentences he uses. Begin *Connie said* ...

1   Connie said _____ .

2   Connie said _____ .

3   Connie said _____ .

4   Connie said _____ .

5   Connie said _____ .

6   Connie said _____ .

Exercise 2   While she was in London, Connie was interviewed in the street by a man from
the British Tourist Authority.
These are some of the questions he asked her.

1   Where are you from?
2   When did you arrive in Britain?
3   Why are you visiting London?
4   How long are you staying?
5   What have you bought in London?
6   Where will you go next?

Later Connie reported these questions to her friend.
Write down the six sentences she used. Begin: *He asked (me)* ...

1 He asked me _____ .

2 He asked me _____ .

3 He asked me _____ .

4 He asked me _____ .

5 He asked me _____ .

6 He asked me _____ .

UNIT 20

Exercise 3   Connie's friend has a brochure about a hotel in York.

Sir Walter Raleigh Hotel, York
- 120 rooms
- £25 per night (including breakfast)
- situated in the centre of town
- 5 minutes walk from railway station
- all rooms have TV, radio and private showers
- our restaurant offers lunch and dinner to our guests
- guided tours of the city every morning and afternoon

Connie is asking her friend about the hotel.
Answer her questions. Begin *It says* ...

Example Is it a big hotel?
Answer It says there are 120 rooms.

1 What about the price?

   It says _____ .

2 Where is the hotel?

   It says _____ .

3 Is it near the railway station?

   It says _____ .

4 What are the rooms like?

   It says _____ .

5 Can we eat at the hotel?

   It says _____ .

6 Do they have any guided tours?

   It says _____ .

Exercise 4   This morning, Mrs Briggs phoned Anna's landlady.
Here are some of the things she said.

1 Anna slept here last night.
2 She went to the cinema with Claude.
3 They got back after 11 o'clock.
4 It was too late to phone you.
5 Anna didn't want to wake you up.
6 She is having some breakfast now.
7 She'll be home after breakfast.

You are Mrs Briggs. Tell Anna what you said on the phone. Begin *I told her* ...

Example I told her that you slept here last night.

1 I told her _____ .

2 I told her _____ .

3 I told her _____ .

4 I told her _____ .

5 I told her _____ .

6 I told her _____ .

Exercise 5   Complete the text with the words in the list. You must use each word only once.

added   after   ago   became   before
by   century   his   royal   until

William I started building Windsor Castle nine hundred years [1]_____ . The original wooden castle was replaced with stone walls [2]_____ Henry II a hundred years later. However, it was not [3]_____ Edward III's reign in the fourteenth [4]_____ that Windsor became the home of the royal family. Henry VIII [5]_____ a new gate and a tennis court to the castle. He is buried there in St George's Chapel. Charles I spent [6]_____ last Christmas as a prisoner at Windsor in 1648 [7]_____ he was executed. Charles II and George IV made improvements to the [8]_____ apartments. Queen Victoria [9]_____ known as 'the Widow of Windsor' because she spent so much time there [10]_____ the death of her husband, Prince Albert.

UNIT 21 Reported Speech II

Exercise 1

George's mother spoke to her husband about George last night. Here are some of the things she said.

1 She said that she couldn't understand George and his friends.
2 She said young people didn't want to work and earn money.
3 She said that George had to work if he wanted money to travel.
4 She told George's father not to give him any more money.
5 She asked George's father why he didn't try to help his son.
6 She asked George's father if he would speak to his son again.

Write down the actual words she said (six sentences).

1 _____ .

2 _____ .

3 _____ .

4 _____ .

5 _____ .

6 _____ .

Exercise 2

George has a friend who works in a travel agency.
He asked him about his job.
Here are his questions.

1 What sort of work do you do?
2 Are you sitting behind a desk all day long?
3 Must you speak foreign languages?
4 How long are the holidays you get?
5 Can you get cheap tickets on flights?
6 Will you get a salary increase soon?

Put these questions into reported speech. Begin each sentence with *George asked his friend* ...

1 George asked his friend _____ .

2 George asked his friend _____ .

3 George asked his friend _____ .

4 George asked his friend _____ .

5 George asked his friend _____ .

6 George asked his friend _____ .

Exercise 3 Put these sentences into reported speech. Begin with:

I	asked	(him) ...
	said	(her) ...
	told	(them) ...

1 Don't worry.
2 You must go immediately.
3 Do you like your job?
4 I'll be home late.

5 It may rain tomorrow.
6 I'm giving a party tonight.
7 I can't drive.
8 Be here by 9 o'clock.

1 _____

2 _____

3 _____

4 _____

5 _____

6 _____

7 _____

8 _____

Exercise 4 George read his horoscope in the newspaper this morning. Now you read it.

> VIRGO 24 August – 23 September
>
> You have been going through a difficult period recently. This week, you will
> have to make an important decision which will affect your future. Discuss
> your plans with your family before you make your decision. You must also
> listen to your friend's advice. This is a good time for travel but there may be
> financial problems.

Put this text into reported speech. Begin with *George's horoscope said that ...*

_____

_____

_____

_____ .

UNIT 21

Exercise 5

Complete the text with the words in the
list. You must use each word only once.

afraid around crowded full going
had last still told waiting

'How long have you been ¹_____ ?' George asked the man in front of him
at the bus stop. He was worried because he was ²_____ to be late for his
first interview. He ³_____ didn't know exactly where the travel agency was.

At ⁴_____ the bus came. The bus was rather ⁵_____ and so the
conductor ⁶_____ George to go upstairs. The windows were all steamed up
and the air was ⁷_____ of tobacco smoke. George was ⁸_____ he would
miss his stop.

When the bus eventually arrived in the town centre, George got off and
looked ⁹_____ him. Finally, he ¹⁰_____ to ask a traffic warden where
the travel agency was.

First Conditional

Exercise 1   Terry ran out of petrol in his new sports car.
There are several things he can do – but there are also problems.

Possibilities	Problems
He can push the car to the garage.	It will take a long time.
He can walk to the garage.	He will probably find it is closed.
He can wait for another car.	He may wait a long time.
He can go to a farm.	They may not have a telephone.
He can take his girl-friend with him.	The car will be unprotected.
He can go by himself.	Muriel will be left alone.
Muriel can go alone.	She might get lost.

Join each pair of sentences, beginning with *If* ...
Example If he pushes the car to the garage, it will take a long time.

1 If _____ .

2 If _____ .

3 If _____ .

4 If _____ .

5 If _____ .

6 If _____ .

Exercise 2   Tom is an English Language Teacher. He has just been offered a post abroad.
Before he accepts the job, he has some questions to ask.

Here are Tom's notes:

Pay return fare ?
Pay family's fares ?
Provide Medical Insurance?
Provide accommodation?
Get work permit ?
Lend money to buy a car ?
Pay children's school ?

Make Tom's questions begin with *If I accept the job* ...
Example If I accept the job, will the company pay for my return fare?

1 _____ .

2 _____ .

3 _____ .

4 _____ .

5 _____ .

6 _____ .

Exercise 3   Make six sentences from this table. Use each phrase once only.

He always switches the radio off He will pass his exam I won't accept the job She practises her English They usually visit us We'll go by boat	unless whenever	he makes stupid mistakes. she gets a chance. the news is on. the seamen are on strike. they increase the salary. they're in London.

1 _____ .

2 _____ .

3 _____ .

4 _____ .

5 _____ .

6 _____ .

Exercise 4   Rewrite these sentences without changing the meaning.

1 I won't tell him if he doesn't ask.

Unless _____ .

2 She always travels first class when she flies to Montreal.

Whenever _____ .

3 We'll have lunch as soon as you have finished.

When _____ .

4 I'll pay this bill unless you object.

If _____ .

5 I'll do the washing up after the programme has finished.

When _____ .

6 They always buy her some champagne on her birthday.

Whenever _____ .

Exercise 5   Complete the text with the words in the list. You must use each word only
once.

another   anything   away   if   manager   paying   replied   tea   will
wouldn't

'But, dear, if we buy our own home, it [1]_____ be an investment.' She
poured James [2]_____ cup of tea. 'At the moment, we're [3]_____ money
for rent which we'll never see again.'

   'That's true,' [4]_____ James. 'But [5]_____ I have to pay a mortgage, we
won't be able to afford holidays abroad. We'll have to move [6]_____ from
the centre of town, too. We couldn't possibly afford to buy [7]_____ near the
centre.'

   'That [8]_____ matter. It's so noisy round here anyway.'

   James stirred his [9]_____ slowly. 'All right,' he said at last, 'I'll go and see
my bank [10]_____ in the morning.'

UNIT 23 The Passive

Exercise 1   Thomas à Becket (1118–1170) was
Archbishop of Canterbury. Here are
some of the facts of his life:

1 1118 born in London
2 1154 became Chancellor of
       England
3 1158 sent to Paris by Henry II
4 1162 made Archbishop of
       Canterbury
5 1164 exiled to France for six years
6 1170 murdered in Canterbury
       Cathedral
7 1173 made a saint by Pope
       Alexander III

Make passive sentences from these notes.
Example Thomas à Becket was born in London in 1118.

1 _____ .

2 _____ .

3 _____ .

4 _____ .

5 _____ .

6 _____ .

7 _____ .

Exercise 2   Answer these with passive sentences.

1 Where is coffee grown?

    _____ Brazil.

2 Where are diamonds mined?

    _____ South Africa.

3 Where is champagne produced?

    _____ France.

4 Where do they make Rolls-Royces?

    _____ Britain.

5 Where can you find Giant Pandas?

    _____ Central China.

6 Is whisky distilled in Scotland?

    _____ Scotland and Ireland.

Exercise 3 Answer these questions about your country.
Use passive sentences.

1 What is the capital city called?

_____ .

2 What fruit is grown in your country?

_____ .

3 Is English taught in the secondary schools?

_____ .

4 Are many commodities exported from your country?

_____ .

5 Describe what sports are played.

_____ .

6 Will your country be represented at the next Olympic Games?

_____ .

Exercise 4 Put the verbs in the correct passive tense.

The development of the English language

Several Saxon dialects _____ (speak)[1] in Britain a thousand years ago.
When the country _____ (convert)[2] to Christianity, Latin

_____ (introduce)[3] by the Church as the language of education.

In the eleventh century, French dialects _____ (bring)[4] from
France by the new ruling class. The English language _____ (develop)[5]
considerably over the next 300 years and by 1383, English was the language
which _____ (use)[6] in the schools.

Original Saxon words _____ (combine)[7] in English with Latin,
Greek and French words. The language _____ (enrich)[8] by many
words and phrases from other foreign languages too.

UNIT 23

Exercise 5   James is telephoning for information about a house he wants to buy. Complete the conversation.

1 JAMES   When _____ ?

HOUSE AGENT   The house was built in 1935.

2 JAMES   I see. And how long _____ ?

HOUSE AGENT   It's been empty since the owner died last year.

3 JAMES   Has central heating _____ ?

HOUSE AGENT   No, central heating hasn't been installed yet.

4 JAMES   And _____ ?

HOUSE AGENT   Yes, it was repainted last year.

5 JAMES   What about the roof?

HOUSE AGENT   I'm afraid the roof _____ yet.

The work will begin next week.

6 JAMES   When _____ ?

HOUSE AGENT   The work will be finished in a month.

70

Phrasal Verbs

Exercise 1 Fill in the spaces with a word from the list.

about   down   off   over   out   through   up

After reading Claire's letter, Ken Mitchell soon got [1]_____ the shock he had received. He set [2]_____ for the office. On the way, the car broke [3]_____ . He was held [4]_____ for an hour while the mechanic was finding [5]_____ what was wrong with the car.

He rang Claire from the office and they talked until they were cut [6]_____ by the switchboard. Ken was very happy that Claire was not going to turn [7]_____ his proposal of marriage after all. He looked [8]_____ several reports on his desk and then decided to go [9]_____ for lunch. In the afternoon, he had a meeting which was called [10]_____ . He cleared [11]_____ the rest of the work on his desk very quickly and left the office early to see [12]_____ some theatre tickets for himself and Claire.

Exercise 2 Revise the list of phrasal verbs on page 141 in your course book. Rewrite these sentences with the correct phrasal verb.

1 She recovered from her illness in six days.

   _____ .

2 A car bomb exploded in Beirut last night.

   _____ .

3 The hijackers surrendered because of the army.

   _____ .

4 The tennis match was postponed because of rain.

   _____ .

5 The plan to build a new stadium failed.

   _____ .

6 The accident occurred on the motorway.

   _____ .

UNIT 24

Exercise 3 You are asking some questions about a dance your friend went to recently.

Make questions from the tables. Your friend's answers are given below the spaces you write in.

What time	did		turn up? break up? held up?
Where	was	the dance	put on? set off?
Why	were	you	take place?

1 _____ ?
To raise money for the village fund.

2 _____ ?
In the village hall.

3 _____ ?
We finished at midnight.

4 _____ ?
We left home at 7.30 pm.

5 _____ ?
I had a puncture.

6 _____ ?
We arrived about 9.00 pm.

Exercise 3 Each of the sentences below contains a phrasal verb. You can guess its meaning from the sentences. Rewrite the sentences with a verb from the list. Make sure you use the correct tense.

explain   find   finish   go to bed   resemble   stop

1 I was very tired so I *turned in* at 10 o'clock.

_____ .

2 I can't *get through* all this work now so I'll do some of it tomorrow.

_____ .

3 He *takes after* his father who used to do exactly the same things.

_____ .

4 I *came across* these old photos in your suitcase.

_____ .

72

5 I have tried to *give up* smoking but I can't.

_____ .

6 I didn't understand the problem so the teacher *went over* it again.

_____ .

Exercise 5   Complete the text with the words in the list. You must use each word only once.

around   back   completely   down   realised   saw   still   suddenly   under   were

He put on his slippers and started [1]_____ the stairs. The lights weren't working so it was [2]_____ dark. At the bottom of the stairs, his feet [3]_____ felt icy cold. He [4]_____ that he was up to his ankles in water. As his eyes grew accustomed to the dark, he [5]_____ that the room was half a meter [6]_____ water. The furniture hadn't moved but some newspapers [7]_____ floating gently across the room. He could hear that it was [8]_____ raining outside.

   At that moment, he felt something cold grip him [9]_____ the ankles. He screamed and ran [10]_____ up the stairs.

UNIT 25 Verbs usually followed by the Gerund

Exercise 1

Imagine you are a football referee.
Make six statements from the table.
Use each verb at least once.

I	(don't)	like	arguing with players.
			playing football.
			refereeing games in the evening.
		like	seeing players pretend to be hurt.
		mind	training hard to keep fit.
			waiting for an important game to begin.

1 _____ .
2 _____ .
3 _____ .
4 _____ .
5 _____ .
6 _____ .

Exercise 2

Look at the example.

Example the concert   listen / classical music
        I'm looking forward to going to the concert.
        I enjoy listening to classical music.

Make similar sentences from these notes.

1 the restaurant   eat / good food

_____ .

2 the match   watch / international football

_____ .

3 the cinema   see / exciting film

_____ .

4 the seaside   swim / the sea

_____ .

5 on holiday   stay / first class hotel

_____ .

6 Scotland   walk / the country

_____ .

Exercise 3   Put the correct verb in these sentences. Use each verb only once. Make sure you use the correct tense.

avoid   consider   deny   finish   keep   miss   suggest   stop

1 He _____ writing the letter until I showed him a copy of it.

2 I _____ smoking when I was thirty.

3 I _____ seeing the play because my car broke down.

4 She _____ ringing the bell until someone answered.

5 My wife and I _____ sending our son to a private school.

6 The car _____ hitting the cyclist by a few centimetres.

7 I _____ moving to the country many times but my husband always refuses.

8 I only _____ painting the door yesterday and now it's dirty again.

Exercise 4   Put these sentences into direct speech.

1 I asked her if she'd mind lending me £5.

_____ .

2 The workmen said they couldn't help making a mess.

_____ .

3 The judge asked her if she denied telling a lie.

_____ .

4 My father told me to stop using the phone before midday.

_____ .

5 The manager said he was considering replacing some of his workmen.

_____ .

6 She asked me if I had finished making the salad.

_____ .

UNIT 25

Exercise 5   Complete the text with the words in the list. You must use each word only once.

can't   enjoy   forward   hate   match   met   part   prevent   think   used

Kenny Dalkeith, the footballer, took ^{1}_____ in Vernon Miller's late night TV show recently.

MILLER   Welcome to the show, Kenny. The last time we ^{2}_____ was at Wembley.

DALKEITH   It was indeed, Vernon. You interviewed me after the ^{3}_____ between Scotland and England last year.

MILLER   Well now, Kenny. You've been in football a long time. Do you still ^{4}_____ playing as much as you ^{5}_____ to?

DALKEITH   Oh yes. I still look ^{6}_____ to going out on the pitch every Saturday. It's been the same ever since I was a kid. I ^{7}_____ stand just watching a game of football. I ^{8}_____ the idea of having to retire one day.

MILLER   What do you ^{9}_____ is the main problem in football these days?

DALKEITH   The violence, of course. Something has to be done to ^{10}_____ the violence both on and off the pitch.

Second Conditional

Exercise 1   David and Laura are thinking of travelling to London. They must choose whether to go by car or by train.

	Journey time	Cost	Advantage	Disadvantage
train	5 hours	£68	quicker	more expensive
car	7 hours	£40	can use the car in London	difficult to park the car in London

Complete these sentences.

1   If they went by train, the journey _____ cost more money.

2   If they took the car, the journey _____ seven hours.

3   They _____ be able to use the car in London if they took it.

4   However, if they _____ by train, the journey _____ much quicker.

5   It _____ an advantage to have the car in London, but they _____ always find it easy to park it.

Exercise 2   Frank is considering buying an old car because it is cheap. But he might need to spend a lot of money on repairs.

Example The tyres are worn. (replace)
        If he bought the car, he would need to replace the tyres.

1   The battery doesn't work. (replace)

_____ .

2   The headlights don't work. (repair)

_____ .

3   It uses a lot of oil. (buy)

_____ .

4   The brakes are weak. (service)

_____ .

5   It is covered with rust. (remove)

_____ .

6   The engine is covered with dirt. (clean)

_____ .

UNIT 26

Exercise 3   Complete these conversations.

Example What / do / be Prime Minister? ... reduce taxes.
What would you do if you were Prime Minister?
If I were Prime Minister, I'd reduce taxes.

1 What / do / win £100,000? ... buy a big house.

_____ .

2 What / do / find a diamond ring? ... take it to the police station.

_____ .

3 Where / live / be a millionaire? ... live in Florida.

_____ .

4 What currency / need / go to New York? ... need US dollars.

_____ .

5 What language / speak / live in Brazil? ... speak Portuguese.

_____ .

6 Who / ask / want to know about computers? ... ask a computer salesman.

_____ .

Exercise 4   Look at the examples.

Example A If you go to London, you will need an umbrella.
THE FIRST CONDITIONAL expresses *possibility*, i.e.
It is quite likely you will go to London.

Example B If Wales became independent, it would be a republic.
The SECOND CONDITIONAL is often used for *unlikely* or *impossible* events.

Complete these sentences (FIRST or SECOND CONDITIONALS)

1 If you _____ (go) to the match next Saturday, you _____
(see) a wonderful game.

2 David _____ (leave) school next month if he _____ (pass)
his exams.

3 If Americans _____ (speak) French, English _____ (not
be) an international language.

4 If computers _____ (not exist), modern business _____
(be) very different.

78

5 If money _____ (grow) on trees, everybody _____ (can be) rich.

6 If the Earth _____ (be) flat, people _____ fall off the edge.

Exercise 5   Complete the text with the words in the list. You must use each word only once.

able   as   came   capital   city   different   from   including   several would

If you visited Scotland, you [1]_____ find it very different from England. The Scottish speak English with [2]_____ accents, all quite different [3]_____ English accents.

The countryside is also quite [4]_____ . There are many more mountains and splendid lakes, known [5]_____ 'lochs'. Some of the lochs, [6]_____ the famous Loch Ness, are very deep.

Edinburgh, the [7]_____ of Scotland, has been called the 'Athens of the North'. It is a very picturesque [8]_____ where many tourists come. If you [9]_____ there in August, you would be [10]_____ to take part in the largest Arts Festival in the world.

UNIT 27 First and Second Conditional Questions

USE DICTIONARY.——

Exercise 1 The solicitor in Unit 27 is not very successful. He would probably be more successful if he changed various things. Find the correct Part B for each Part A. Do not change the order of the sentences under Part A.

Part A	Part B
1 He would save some money	he could charge higher fees.
2 He would attract more clients	he would have more time to take care of important clients.
3 If he had more clients,	if he charged higher fees.
4 If he attracted prosperous clients	if he moved to more fashionable premises.
5 He could afford to get an assistant	if he only had one secretary.
6 If he had an assistant,	some of them would be more prosperous

1 _____ .

2 _____ .

3 _____ .

4 _____ .

5 _____ .

6 _____ .

Exercise 2 You are considering buying a house in Britain. You would have to get a loan from a bank. Form questions you would ask the bank manager from this table. His answers are given below the spaces that you write in.

How How long How much How often What Who	would	I you	ask to examine the house? calculate the amount of my loan? have to make repayments? have to pay back the loan? have to pay in interest? want as security for the loan?

1 _____ ?

We can lend you up to three times your annual salary.

2 _____ ?

You could pay it back over 15–25 years.

3 _____?

The interest rate at the moment is 11 per cent a year.

4 _____?

We normally ask our customers to make monthly repayments.

5 _____?

The house itself would act as security for the loan.

6 _____?

Our surveyor would examine the house for you.

Exercise 3   Gertrude and Jim are going on a camping holiday in France. Their parents are worried and they have some questions. Ask and answer their questions from the tables.

What will you do if	1 people can't speak English? 2 you get ill? 3 you run out of money? 4 your things are stolen? 5 the camp sites are full? 6 the weather is bad?

If _____ , we'll	go and see our friends in Paris. go to a doctor. go to the local police. stay in a cheap hotel. use French of course. use our Eurocheque cards.

1 _____.

2 _____.

3 _____.

4 _____.

5 _____.

6 _____.

UNIT 27

Exercise 4   David Renton is considering giving up his job and moving to the country. His manager has some questions to ask him. Make questions and answers from the notes. Use SHOULD, WOULD or COULD.

1 MANAGER   When / want / leave / job?

   _____ .

   DAVID   I / give notice / next spring.

   _____ .

2 MANAGER   How much / need / buy / smallholding?

   _____ .

   DAVID   I / need / about £50 000.

   _____ .

3 MANAGER   How / sell / vegetables?

   _____ .

   DAVID   sell / local shops and restaurants.

   _____ .

4 MANAGER   What / wife / do?

   _____ .

   DAVID   work / pub / nearby village.

   _____ .

5 MANAGER   Where / children / go / school?

   _____ .

   DAVID   go / local school.

   _____ .

6 MANAGER   think / earn enough to survive?

   _____ .

   DAVID   sure / earn at least £5000 a year.

   _____ .

Exercise 5   Complete the text with the words in the list. You must use each word once only.

all asked could have if pension replied were would wouldn't

I once asked a farmer what he would like to be [1]_____ he weren't a farmer.

'An office worker', he [2]_____ immediately.

'Why [3]_____ you want to be an office worker?' I asked.

'Well, if I [4]_____ an office worker, I wouldn't [5]_____ to work seven days a week. I [6]_____ have holidays without worrying about animals and the weather all the time. I would retire on a nice big [7]_____ when I was 65.'

'[8]_____ you miss all this fresh air if you moved to the city?' I [9]_____

'I've had [10]_____ the fresh air I want, thank you,' he answered bluntly.

UNIT 28 Must have ... / Should have ...

Exercise 1
Read 'My Grandfather's Watch' on page 161 again. Make six true statements from the table below.

Grandfather The man in the cloth cap	must should have shouldn't	kept his overcoat buttoned up. let anybody see his gold watch. read the advertisement in the paper. reported the theft to the police. stolen the watch a second time. trusted the man in the cloth cap.

1 _____ .

2 _____ .

3 _____ .

4 _____ .

5 _____ .

6 _____ .

Exercise 2
Some valuable paintings were stolen from an art gallery last night. The manager is talking to the police. Complete the conversation with the expressions in the list. Use each expression only once.

might have   must have   must have been   can't have   should have
shouldn't have

POLICEMAN   The thieves [1]_____ got into the gallery during the
night because none of the windows are broken.

MANAGER   You mean they [2]_____ come in before we closed
yesterday evening.

POLICEMAN   Yes, they [3]_____ hiding somewhere in the gallery
when everybody went home. Your staff [4]_____
inspected the gallery more carefully before going home. They
[5]_____ allowed anyone to remain in the gallery. Or,
possibly, one of your staff [6]_____ let the thieves in
with his key ...

Exercise 3   Use the expression in brackets to make a comment about each situation.

1   Carla has lost her camera. Unfortunately, it isn't insured. (should have)

_____ .

2   Fred becomes very ill when he drinks whisky. Last night he drank half a bottle. (shouldn't have)

_____ .

3   You are supposed to meet a friend at the airport. She is coming from New York. The plane from New York arrived an hour ago but she hasn't turned up. (must have)

_____ .

4   When you returned home from holiday, you found all the lights in your house were on. You had told your son to look after the house. (can't have)

_____ .

5   You find an old woman lying injured at the bottom of a cliff. She has some flowers in her hand like those which grow at the edge of the cliff. (must have)

_____ .

6   Mrs Taylor is worried. Her husband forgot his glasses this morning and he is driving home. He should have arrived an hour ago. (might have)

_____ .

Exercise 4   Complete these sentences with an expression which includes SHOULD NEVER

1   It was wrong of her to accept the job.

She _____ the job.

2   It was wrong of her to move out of London.

She _____ .

3   It was wrong of him to destroy the painting.

He _____ the painting.

4   It was wrong of me to borrow the car.

I _____ the car.

5   It was wrong of you to lend him so much money.

You _____ so much money.

6   It was wrong of Frank to take the keys.

Frank _____ the keys.

UNIT 28

Exercise 5   Complete the text with the words in the list. You must use each word only once.

became   have   in   joined   life   managed   on   saw   travelled   was

Churchill had a very eventful [1]_____ even before he first entered Parliament in 1900. He [2]_____ an army officer in 1895. He first saw a battle [3]_____ his twenty-first birthday during a rebellion [4]_____ Cuba. He served in the army in India and [5]_____ a lot of fighting there. After India, he [6]_____ a famous military expedition which was sent to Khartoum in Sudan. When he returned from this expedition, he [7]_____ to South Africa to write newspaper articles about the Boer War. He [8]_____ captured by the enemy but he managed to escape.

During these five years (1895–1900), he also [9]_____ to write several books. He must [10]_____ had a lot of stamina.

Third Conditional UNIT 29

Exercise 1   Read 'The Man who missed the Plane' on page 168 again. Then find the right Part A to go with each Part B in the table. Do not change the order of the Part A's.

Part A	Part B
1 The TV company wouldn't have bought the play	he wouldn't have been invited to New York.
2 If the Americans hadn't decided to produce it,	he would have been killed in the crash.
3 If he had wound up his alarm clock,	he wouldn't have overslept.
4 He would have caught the plane	if he hadn't wanted to check the time.
5 If he had caught the plane,	if it hadn't been so successful.
6 He wouldn't have turned on and heard the news	if the taxi driver hadn't overslept.

1 _____ .
2 _____ .
3 _____ .
4 _____ .
5 _____ .
6 _____ .

Exercise 2   Reply to these comments with a THIRD CONDITIONAL question.

1 I wouldn't have bought that kind of car.

Which _____ ?

2 You should have told your father.

Why _____ ?

3 I would have painted it a different colour.

What _____ ?

4 You shouldn't have done it like that.

How _____ ?

UNIT 29

5 You must have been mad to ask him. He's useless.

Who _____ ?

6 You shouldn't have taken it out of the oven so soon.

How long _____ ?

Exercise 3 The THIRD CONDITIONAL is often used when we are being 'wise after the event'. Make a THIRD CONDITIONAL sentence from each set of statements.

Example I was late. I got the sack.
                 If I hadn't been late, I wouldn't have got the sack.

1 His car broke down. He missed the match.

_____ .

2 It rained. He caught a cold.

_____ .

3 She broke her leg. She went skiing.

_____ .

4 I didn't see the advertisement. I didn't apply for the job.

_____ .

5 I wasn't there. I didn't take her to hospital.

_____ .

6 You reminded me of the appointment. I didn't forget it.

_____ .

Exercise 4 Put the verbs in brackets in the correct tenses. Be careful. They may be FIRST, SECOND or THIRD CONDITIONAL sentences.

1 You were wrong to shout at him. I _____ (apologise) if I

_____ (be) you.

2 We just missed the train. If we _____ (be) five minutes earlier, we

_____ (catch) it.

3 Hold it properly. It _____ (break) if you _____ (not be)

careful.

4 He failed his exam. If he _____ (get) one more mark, he

_____ (pass) it.

5 I'm fed up with waiting. If the bus _____ (not come) soon, we

_____ (get) a taxi.

6 We _____ (go) by car. If I _____ (have) one. I sold mine

yesterday.

Exercise 5 Complete the text with the words in the list. You must use each word only once.

been   eating   gave   had   immediately   left   lying   news   thinking
would

After he [1]_____ listened to the news, James lit a cigarette and sat down. If

there had [2]_____ any brandy in the house, he would have had a large glass.

He certainly didn't feel like [3]_____ any breakfast. He tried to stop

[4]_____ about the plane crash. His ticket was still [5]_____ on top of his

passport where he had [6]_____ it the night before. At ten o'clock, he

listened to the [7]_____ again. The announcer [8]_____ some more

details about the crash. The pilot had reported two engines out of order almost

[9]_____ after take-off. If only one engine had failed, the plane [10]_____

never have crashed.

UNIT 30 To Have / Get Something Done

Exercise 1 Mr Baker did all his own repairs, but he wasn't very good at repairing things. Make sentences from the notes.

Example repainted / decorator
　　　　　Mr Baker should have had (got) his flat repainted by a decorator.

1 rewired / electrician

　　_____ .

2 walls repaired / plasterer

　　_____ .

3 walls tiled / builder

　　_____ .

4 walls papered / decorator

　　_____ .

5 cupboards made / carpenter

　　_____ .

6 plumbing done / plumber

　　_____ .

Exercise 2 Make questions to complete these short conversations.

1 A I had my hair cut yesterday.

　 B Where did you have _____ ?

　 A In London.

2 A Peter had his car repaired at that new garage.

　 B When _____ ?

　 A Last week.

3 A Jim got the builders to repair the roof.

　 B Why _____ ?

　 A Because it was leaking.

4 A Sally got some of the photos enlarged.

　 B Which ones _____ ?

　 A The ones she took on holiday.

5 A Sean got his chest X-rayed last week.

  B Why _____ ?

  A Because he needs a medical certificate.

6 A Debbie had her teeth done by that Polish dentist.

  B What _____ to her teeth?

  A He only cleaned and polished them.

Exercise 3 Mr Renton took his car to the garage
for repairs. Here is the bill he received.

AUTOCARE LTD	£	p
to recharge the battery	5	50
to fit new spark plugs	8	90
to check the engine	17	50
to balance the wheels	9	60
to change the oil	10	50
to service the brakes	22	00
	64	00
VAT @ 15%	9	60
	£73	60

What did Mr Renton have done to
his car?

1 _____ recharged.

2 _____ fitted.

3 _____ checked.

4 _____ wheels _____ .

5 _____ oil _____ .

6 _____ brakes _____ .

Exercise 4 Look at Mr Renton's bill again.
Complete the questions.

1 'How much did it cost _____ recharged?'
  '£5:50.'

2 'How much _____ ?'
  '£10:50.'

3 'What did he _____ to the engine?'
  'He only had it checked.'

4 'What _____ ?'
  'He had them balanced.'

5 'Why did he _____ ?'
  'Because the old ones were worn out.'

6 'Where _____ ?'
  'At Autocare Ltd.'

UNIT 30

Exercise 5   Revise the IRREGULAR VERBS on page 178. Complete each of these sentences with one IRREGULAR VERB from page 178. Make sure you choose the correct verb form.

1 In 1981, I _____ to Bahrain on Concorde.

2 Before he went to bed, he _____ up his alarm clock.

3 In Europe, English is _____ in most secondary schools.

4 I had never _____ of Picasso before I went to Art College.

5 Coffee has been _____ in Brazil for many years.

6 He _____ all his money on a new TV set.

7 I have never _____ *'Das Kapital'* by Karl Marx.

8 Sheila _____ her guitar with her to the party.

9 After he had _____ down the stairs, he lay on the floor for a long time.

10 The Qur'an is _____ in Classical Arabic.